Games for all Seasons   2

Treasure Hunt

Before setting out on a car journey, make a list of things to track down along the road, such as a broken-down car, a burned-out house, a woman wearing a purple dress and yellow hat, a cartload of hay, a Great Dane, a pale blue cowshed, and so on. Include some difficult things, like a horse with a bandaged leg or a church with three windows. Cross off the things as you find them.

This is just one of the numerous games you can have fun with which you can find in this book.

3 bcd

Other books edited by E. Bompiani

GAMES FOR ALL SEASONS 1

and published by CAROUSEL BOOKS

GAMES FOR ALL SEASONS. BOOK TWO
A CAROUSEL BOOK 0 552 54088 9

Originally published in Great Britain by
Methuen Children's Books Ltd.

Originally published in Italy 1971
by Casa Editrice Valentino Bompiano & C
as 'Io Gioco, Tu Giochi, Noi Giochiamo'

PRINTING HISTORY
Methuen edition published 1973
Carousel edition published 1975

Carousel Books are published by Transworld Publishers, Ltd, Cavendish House, 57-59
Uxbridge Road, Ealing, London W5.

Printed by James Paton Ltd, Paisley.

GAMES FOR ALL SEASONS

Book Two

Edited by EMANUELA BOMPIANI

Illustrations and design by ALFREDO DE SANTIS
Translated from the Italian by SYLVIA MULCAHY
With the collaboration of CARLO BRIZZOLARA, GIOVANELLA
DEL PANTA, IPPOLITO PIZZETTI

Consultant editor: Anne Wood

CAROUSEL BOOKS
A DIVISION OF TRANSWORLD PUBLISHERS LTD

Games for all seasons is a collection of nearly 270 games, to play alone or with friends, indoors or out, at any time and in any place. A few of the games will already be familiar to some readers, but most of them—collected from all over the world—will be completely new. All the games have been divided into sections—Games for a rainy day, Creative games, and so on—and there is a full index at the end so that you can easily pick out the most suitable one for any particular occasion. At the beginning of each game is a series of symbols which can be explained as follows:

The sun means that the game is to be played outdoors
The roof means that it is to be played indoors
The numbers, which run from one to twelve, indicate in bold figures the age-range for which the game is most suitable. The example on the right shows that it is for children from seven to eleven years of age

One dot means that the game is to be played by one player
Two dots means that it is for two children
Three dots means that several children can play the game

When you have chosen a game, read the instructions carefully then gather together everything needed (most things can be found around the house); if necessary, each game can be adapted to suit different requirements and abilities.
You will find that this collection is a mine of ideas for games for playing on your own or in a group, when it rains or when you have to stay in bed with a cold, when you can play in the garden or when you have to stay in the car for hours and hours. It is truly a book of games for all seasons.

1234
5678
9101112

•   ••   •••••
          ••

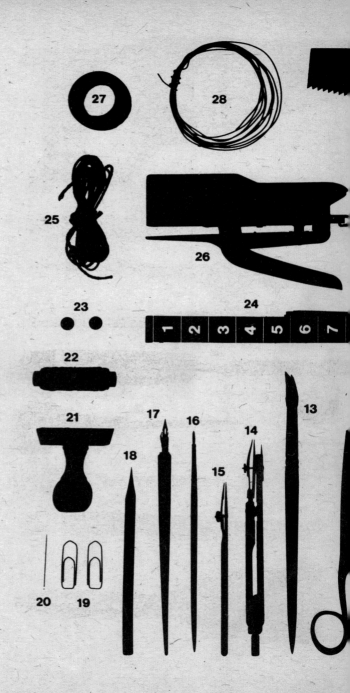

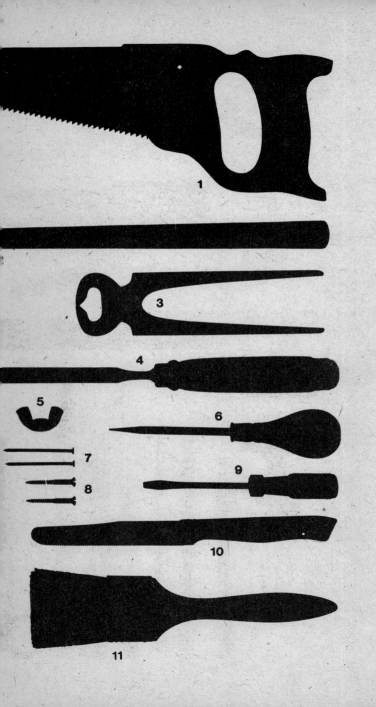

INTRODUCTION

Tools you may need

1	Saw	15	Drawing pen (for ruling lines)
2	Hammer	16	Fine paintbrush
3	Pincers	17	Pen
4	Chisel	18	Pencil
5	Wing nuts	19	Paperclips
6	Prick-punch	20	Needle
7	Nails	21	Rubber stamp and ink pad
8	Screws	22	Cotton
9	Screwdriver	23	Drawing pins
10	Knife	24	Tape measure
11	Flat glue brush	25	String
12	Scissors	26	Stapler
13	Paintbrush	27	Adhesive tape
14	Compass	28	Wire

Gluing

Before starting to glue anything, put a sheet of paper on your working surface.
Everything to be glued must always be clean and dry.
Before gluing smooth surfaces, lightly sandpaper the parts to be stuck together. Never use too much glue.
After sticking paper together, or photographs, leaves, flowers, etc., on to paper, protect it with some clean paper and let it dry out flat under a weight of some sort.
Clean up any drops of glue while still wet.

Painting

Before starting painting, put a sheet of paper on your working surface. If using a spray paint, protect everything around (furniture, walls, etc.) with old newspapers.
Primary colours are easier to apply and brighter than secondary colours.
All surfaces to be painted must be clean, free from grease (you can make sure of this by cleaning with a little white spirit or acetone) and completely dry. Do not apply a second coat until the first is dry.
Leave the painted object to dry in a place where there is no dust and well away from any source of heat.
Place eggs, balls, and anything circular in the hole of an inverted flowerpot to keep them steady while painting.
Clean up spots of paint while they are still wet with water, white spirit or turpentine substitute, according to the type of paint. Always wash brushes well after use.

Materials	Glues	Colours
Wood	Vinavyl	Paint
Plywood	Vinavyl	Paint
Paper	Cow gum	Water colours
Cardboard	Uhu	Water colours
Cloth	Copydex	Silca
Iron	Bostik	Paint
Glass	Uhu	Enamel paint

Games for
a car journey

Before starting this chapter, there are some basic rules, common to all car games, which everyone must know:

1   remain sitting down;
2   never touch or bump up against the driver;
3   don't make a noise.

1234 ●●●●●
5678 ●●
9 10 11 12

Animals and Vegetables

If you are travelling through country very different from where you come from as far as plants and animal life are concerned, write down the name of every type of animal and plant that you see and are able to recognize.

1234 ●●●●●
5678 ●●
9 10 11 12

Who Lives There?

Pick out a house that you see along the road, a rather unusual sort of house, and then try—with the help of a little imagination—to describe what it looks like inside—the walls, floors, number of rooms, furniture, etc.—and who the people are that live there—how the family is made up, what work they do, what they look like, their characters, etc.

The same game can be played by selecting a car or even a whole village. You might ask each other how many years it has existed; how many inhabitants there are; how they live; what the main resources of the village are; what its origin is; and so on.

The state of the roads, the number and appearance of the shops and hotels, the cultivation of the fields, the presence of factory chimneys, the density of traffic, and many other signs indicate whether it is a tourist centre or an industrial or agricultural area and how important it is. Look out for all these things, and for others as well, and put them together with your own imagination.

km

10

Time and Distance

When you are going along a stretch of road where you can see quite a long way ahead, choose a point of reference along the road and try to guess how far away it is—it may be a water reservoir, a bridge, cattle or any other object you like—and how long it will take to reach it.

Now look at the speedometer, make a note of the mileage it shows and of the time. A prize of two pence is awarded to the child whose two calculations are right, a penny to the child who is fairly close with both answers and a halfpenny to the one who is fairly close with only one answer. The prize might be doubled if anyone gets both calculations exactly right.

Animal Hunt

In this game, different values are given to different animals. A dog, for example, might be worth one point, a cat two points, a chicken three, a swallow four, and so on. The list will have to be changed from district to district and so the value of the animals must also be altered—animals which are less likely to be found in certain areas will have a higher value than the more common ones.

The players divide into two groups and each group looks out for the animals on its own side of the road only. If an animal crosses the road, it belongs to whoever saw it first. The first to reach 50 or 100 points is the winner.

The Route Official.

Each child has a road map of the area to be covered during the journey. Before starting out, they draw their route in ink, marking with a small circle or star the point of departure, the main deviations, the places (if any) where it is intended to stop, one or two points of reference (rivers, lakes, castles, woods, etc.) and the destination. During the drive, each child will be able to keep up to date with his position, tracing a line in pencil along the road covered and checking, from time to time, the points which have been marked before setting out.

Word Splitting

Any word may be chosen provided it is very long— marvellously, for example. Each player writes it down on a piece of paper. The game consists in making as many words as possible from the letters in it. The winner is the one to find most words within a prearranged time.

"If he were . . .?"

One of the children stops up his ears while the others, in low voices, select a well-known character, dead or alive. When they have agreed on who it shall be—let us say they have chosen Christopher Columbus—the one who has to guess who it is starts by asking each of the other players a question, such as "If he were a means of transport what would he be?" The answer must bear some relation to the character and so he could say, "A ship". The next question and answer might be: "If he were a book what would he be?" "He would be a log book." And so it goes on until the personality has been guessed within a prearranged time limit.

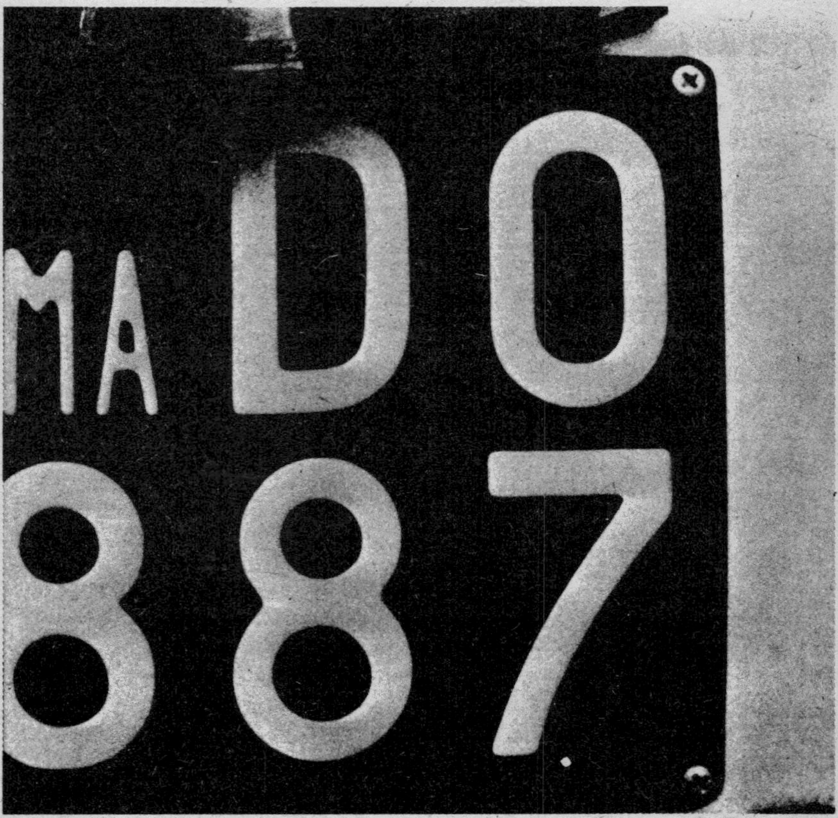
MA DO
887

Names of . . . .

This game is played to a rhythm of 1–2–3–4, which is made by clapping hands, slapping knees, snapping the fingers of the right hand and then the left, in chorus. Each group of beats should sound more or less like this: clap, clap, snap, snap. Each player in turn chooses a category in which the others must find as many names as possible, without losing the 1–2–3–4 rhythm. The best way to explain is to give an example:

1st player (clap, clap, snap, snap): Names of . . . wild
flowers
2nd player   „   „   „   „ Dandelion
3rd player   „   „   „   „ Daisy
4th player   „   „   „   „ Groundsel

and so on, one after the other. Words which have already been said cannot be used again. A player who repeats a word or who makes a mistake is out of the game. The winner is the last one to be left in.

Naturally the names of anything can be used—masculine and feminine first names, footballers, cars, cities, friends, famous men, etc.

NUMBER PLATES

Numbers in Order

This game can be played by yourself or in competition with others. Start by looking for a number plate with the figure 1, then 2, 3, 4, etc. Obviously the task becomes more difficult when two-digit number have to be found. A time limit or a goal of 50, 100, 253, or any figure you choose, can be set.

A variation of this game permits the players to use any number they may see along the road, not only those on number plates.

Choosing a Number

Choose a three-figure number, such as 967. The game is to try to find the same figures on a number plate, either in the original order or jumbled up (796, for instance). Award 1 point for each version and 5 points for the exact number. The first to reach 10 points is the winner.
Variation: A point could be gained for the number plate: with the lowest number encountered on a particular stretch of road;
with two or three of the same figures;
for figures that appear in a line in the correct order or in any sequence (345, 876, 135) or reversible (363).

Word Making

Choose a name such as the name of one of the children in the car or the name of the next town. Try to make it up from the letters on the number plates you see, in the right order of course. For instance, for "Richard" first R then I then C, etc. Decide before you start when the game should end (if you are making up the name of the next city, you might decide to complete it before getting there, for instance).
To make this game more exciting, and especially if you are scoring points, make up more than one name at a time. Why not make up the names of everyone in the car?

RICH
ARD

ZYXWV
UTSRQP
ONMLK
JIHGF
EDCBA

The Alphabet

Each child plays on his own, looking for the letters of the alphabet in their correct order on number plates and road signs. First A then B then C, and so on. The one to finish the alphabet first is the winner. This game is based on honesty because the only way to win is to spot letters that the others have missed. The game should not be interrupted until it has reached the end.

Here are two variations:
1 make up the alphabet backwards;
2 limit the game solely to number plates.

Letters and Words

Another game can be played by using the letters of number plates instead of the numbers. The purpose is to make up the longest possible words which include the letters in the same order in which they appear on the number plates. For instance, from DOY you might make inDicatOrY, DictiOnarY, enDOgamY, or from FXN FiXatioN, inFleXioN, reFleXioN.
You might stipulate that the word must start with the first letter on the number plate or alternatively that it must *not* start with that letter. After the various combinations have been exhausted, the game can be continued by turning the same letters round so that DOY and FXN become YOD and NXF until the prearranged score has been reached.

1234
5678
9 10 11 12

Proverbs

Each player in turn must repeat as many proverbs as he can remember. The same game can be played with everyday sayings such as, "Pretty as a picture", "Stubborn as a mule", etc.

Car Identification

This is a game suitable for car enthusiasts. Each player in turn challenges the others to identify a car. A point is lost for every mistake and the first to lose, say, 10 points is out of the game. The challenger must be able to identify the car correctly himself and if the challenged player is unable to identify it he can ask the challenger to do so— the latter will lose a point if he gives an incorrect answer.

Make and Date

This variation is reserved for the experts: the game is basically the same as the previous one, with the difference that the year in which the model first came on to the market must be given as well as the other specifications.

Story Roundabout

In this roundabout everyone tells part of a story. Each passenger is allowed a given amount of time to think of a story (they should try to get inspiration to start the story from something seen during the journey). When the first narrator has exhausted his allotted time, the second goes on with it from the point at which it has been left, and so on.

The game can be varied by introducing the rule that when a player comes to the end of his time he must look out of the window and select some object that he sees there and the following player must incorporate it in his part of the story.

The story can be made to last as long as you want, that is to say until it reaches its natural conclusion or until it reaches the point of being so desperately complicated that it is simply impossible to continue.

1 2 3 4
5 6 7 8
9 10 11 **12**

Botticelli

This, and the game that follows, are for older children, let us say those from twelve years old.

One of the players chooses a character, alive or dead, and tells the others the initial letter of his or her surname. For example, if he decides on Botticelli, the letter would be B. Then the others start to put their questions, more or less like this:

"Is he a composer?" The first player must not simply reply "No", but must add that the character is not Bach, Brahms, Beethoven or Berlioz (that is, the name of any composer whose surname starts with B).

"Is he a writer?" 'No, he is not Butler, Buck," etc.

"Is he a footballer?" "No, he is not Best," etc.

If the player being questioned is not able to think of a name starting with B but the person who has put the question *is* able to find one, the latter can then ask a question to which only "Yes" or "No" can be answered. For example, "Is he still alive?" "No."

The game continues until the character's identity has been discovered.

The Beaver

Choose a subject—for instance, a man wearing braces—who will be called "beaver". A player gains 1 point each time he is the first to spot the beaver, in this case a man with braces. When a beaver has been pointed out, no other player can claim him. One point is lost for repetitions or for inexact spotting.

Let us pretend that a particular white car has been chosen as your beaver and that, while you are overtaking one, one of the players calls out and claims it as his beaver. From that moment, everyone must be on the look-out for that sort of white car. If the same white car overtakes you and a player claims it, he would lose a point.

Or let us imagine that the beaver is a house that has no curtains to be seen from the street. As you pass one, someone calls out "Beaver!" because no curtains are visible on the side of the house facing you. But if, when you have passed it, you can see curtains on the side, the player who claimed it will have to lose a point.

Signs

This game consists of discovering strange names of hotels, restaurants or public houses along the road.

The passengers in the car agree on a certain number of points to be won for each sign. The *Chamois Hotel* or the *Balmy Restaurant* might be worth only a few points, but how many would you award for a public house called *The Blue-haired Witch*, *The Zig-Zag Arms*, or *The Bald-faced Stag*?

The Sleeping Giant

We often see something in nature that makes us think of something else. We have all seen trees that the wind, or some natural malformation, has twisted into strange shapes—one may resemble a man bowing, another is like a woman waving to a friend in the distance, or two trees may look as though they are shaking hands or even about to come to blows. Rocks and clouds can take on the shapes of human faces, castles and towers, and a range of hills can make us think of a woman or a sleeping giant. It can be great fun discovering these different shapes in the countryside, as we pass through, and to give them imaginary names. In this game there are no points to be won—only the appreciation of the others!

Treasure Hunt

Before setting out, make a list of things to track down along the road, such as a broken-down car, a burned-out house, a woman wearing a purple dress and yellow hat, a cartload of hay, a Great Dane, a pale blue cowshed, and so on. Do not make the list too long; thirty items will be more than enough. However, it is a good idea to make it in such a way as to include some difficult things, like a horse with a bandaged leg or a church with three windows. Take the list with you and cross off the things as you find them. The ones left can be used on the next journey.

The Ghost

In this game, words have to be made up but the whole purpose is *not* to complete them. One of the players suggests a letter of the alphabet and the next player suggests another. If a player adds a letter which, added to the others, makes a proper word, he becomes part of a "ghost", that is, each time he slips up he must mark against himself the letters G, H, O, S and T until he has become a complete ghost and is eliminated from the game.

When a player adds a letter, he must have a word already in mind in which this letter would fit. For example, if someone adds a Q to LES, the player who follows would be right to doubt that such a word exists and should challenge the previous player. If the latter cannot prove the existence of such a word, he must add a letter to his own ghost.

The main object is to try to force someone *else* to finish the word as well as avoiding being forced to do so yourself. For example, if you add an R to PURPO, the next player could add a T to make the word PURPORT, which will cost him a letter in his ghost.

The Box

1234
5678
9101112

Two or more children make several lines of dots on a sheet of paper—it is up to them to decide how many lines and how many dots. At first, it is best to start with four lines with five dots in each line.

Each player, in turn, joins together two dots by drawing a horizontal or vertical line between them. The object of the game is to prevent your opponent from closing the fourth side of a box.

You will see from the diagram how the game looks on paper in a duel in which each player has had six turns. It will soon be impossible to avoid a box being closed.

As soon as a player succeeds in closing a box, he writes his initials in it and stays in play, closing as many boxes as he can. If it is not possible to close any more, he draws a line on another part of the design. When all the boxes are closed, the winner is the one whose initials appear most often.

GHO
ST

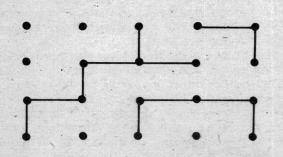

Party
games

Games marked with an asterisk * are for children in pairs.

What Is My Name?

1 2 3 4
5 **6 7 8**
9 10 11 12

This game is very good for getting a party started.
Before your guests arrive, write the names of everyone
in large letters on a piece of white cardboard. Cut the
cardboard in two, separating the first name from the
surname and then cut all the names out. Attach a safety-
pin to each one and hide them all round the house. When
the children arrive, they must hunt for *both* parts of their
name. When they find one part, they can pin it on their
chest and then continue the search until they have found
the other part too.

County, City, River, Landmark . . . .

1 2 3 4
5 6 7 **8**
9 10 11 12

This can also be a good way of dividing the children
into teams. Give each of them the name of a country, a
city, a river, a landmark, etc. The players who have been
given the name of a country have to join up with those
who have the name of a city, river, etc., which belongs
to it. Here are a few examples:

Country	City	River	Landmark
England	London	Thames	Big Ben
France	Paris	Seine	Eiffel Tower
Italy	Pisa	Arno	Leaning Tower
Scotland	Glasgow	Clyde	Kelvin Hall
Russia	Moscow	Volga	Kremlin
USA	New York	Hudson	Statue of Liberty
Egypt	Cairo	Nile	Sphinx

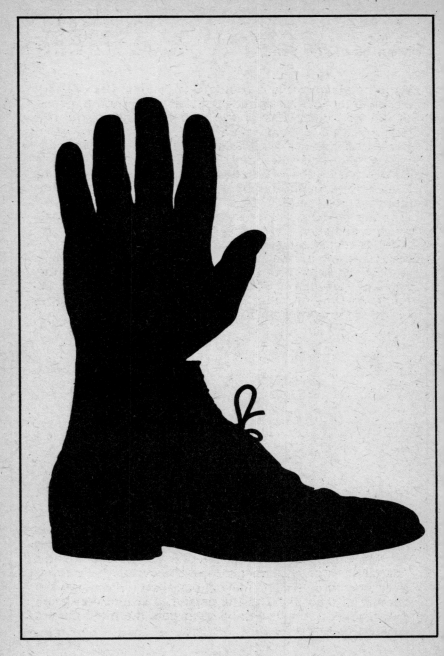

Months of the Year

Write on pieces of card about 10 cm square ($3\frac{1}{2} \times 3\frac{1}{2}$ in.) all the letters of the alphabet needed to write the names of the twelve months of the year (and include all the letters that appear more than once).

Divide the children into two, three or four teams (according to how many there are) and give one letter to each child. If there are any letters over, distribute them equally between the teams, in which case some players will have more than one card.

Line the teams up along one wall of the room and call out the names of the twelve months either in their right order or mixed up. As each month is called, the players who have any of the letters in it must run to the opposite wall of the room and line up in their team to form the name of that month. The team that finishes first wins 10 points and the one that gets the most points at the end of the game wins a prize.

Mysterious Hands

Make a curtain with an old sheet, paper or any other suitable material and make some holes in it, numbering the holes, through which the children can put their hands. The children on the other side of the curtain have to try to recognize them. The players can then write down the number of the hand and the person to whom they think the hands belong. The child who gets the most correct answers wins a prize.

*Twin Ribbons

Cut up some ribbons in pairs of different lengths, for example two pieces of 20 cm (7 in.), two pieces of 25 cm (10 in.) and two pieces of 30 cm (12 in.), according to the number of children invited. Jumble the ribbons up and get them well tangled—but not too tightly. Each player then has to pull one out of the pile and his partner will be the child who has found the other ribbon of the pair.

Journalism

Give each child a piece of paper and a pencil. Each one must then write a list of the most important events that have taken place during the course of the year. The winner will be the player to have written down the greatest number—but it is always fun to read the others' lists too.

41

Car Identification

Cut out some pictures of cars from newspapers and
magazines, number them and hang them round the room.
Give every child a sheet of paper and a pencil. He will
then guess the make of each car, writing its name by the
side of the corresponding number. The one who gets the
most right is the winner.

*Topping-up

Divide the players into pairs consisting of a boy and a
girl. Give each girl a glass of water and a spoon. Her job
is to give the water to her partner, spooning it into his
mouth. The winners are the pair who empty the glass
first.

Balloon Race

The players in each team spread out in well-spaced lines.
The first child in every line is given a balloon which he
must throw up into the air towards the second player in
his team. It does not matter if the balloon is touched more
than once—the important thing is for it to stay in the air.
The balloon is passed all the way back along the line, in
this way, from one player to the next, and then returned
to the first child by the same means. Any team who lets
the balloon fall must start again from the beginning. The
winning team is the one that is first to bring the balloon
back to the starting point.

Catch the Whistler!

A piece of string about 1 m (3 ft.) long is attached to the back of the "blind fly", with a whistle tied on the end of it. The players divide into two teams and each player must try to blow the whistle without letting himself be touched by the "blind fly". If he succeeds, he gains 3 points for his team but if he gets touched then the team loses a point. The winners are the team to reach 20 points first.

The Sculptor

Before starting work, the sculptor announces what expression he wants to give his creations. For example he may say, "I want to create the most graceful of statues," or the most frightening, or the most ridiculous, and so on. When he has said this, he gets hold of each player by the hand, turns him round and round and then suddenly lets go. The "statue" must immediately take up his pose in the necessary position and with the relevant expression. When all the "statues" have been "sculptured", the artist chooses the best one, his masterpiece, which then becomes the new sculptor.

*Cops and Robbers

Two players are chosen by casting lots—one will be the cop and the other the robber. Both are blindfolded and led to the two ends of a table. To play this game successfully, it is necessary to listen very hard and to walk on tip-toe. The cop has to try to catch the robber and the robber has to try to keep well clear of him. Both of them must always keep one hand on the table. If the robber has not been captured in three minutes, he becomes the cop and lots are cast for another child to become the robber. If, however, the robber has been caught, then both players are replaced.

Blow-ball

The players are divided into two teams. The first player in both teams kneels down in front of a tape that marks the starting line. They are both given a ping-pong ball and a drinking-straw. At the word "Off!", they put the ball down on the ground in front of them and blow it through the straw to make it roll across the floor until it reaches the finishing line (another strip of tape). As soon as a child has blown his ball over the finishing line he picks it up and races back to the second player in his team who is waiting with his straw at the ready. When the second player receives the ball, he sets off in the same way. The winning team is the one whose players finish first.

47

Bean Race

The players line up in two teams. Place a spoon, a small container and ten beans on the ground a few feet in front of the first players. At the word "Go!", the first child in each team runs up to the spoon and puts the beans, one at a time, into the container using the spoon and one hand only. When all ten beans have been collected they must be turned out again on the ground and everything left in place, just as before. The player then runs back to his team so that the second one—who in the meantime has taken up his place on the starting line—can set off right away. The winning team is the one whose members finish first.

The Flying Puff-ball

All the children sit on the ground in as tight a circle as possible. One of them throws a small ball of cotton wool into the air and blows upwards, from underneath, to keep it airborne. Then the nearest player blows it towards another child and so on. Anyone who lets it fall to the ground must pay a forfeit. It will be worst for anyone who laughs just at the moment of blowing or for anyone who breathes too hard—he risks finding himself with a mouthful of cotton wool!

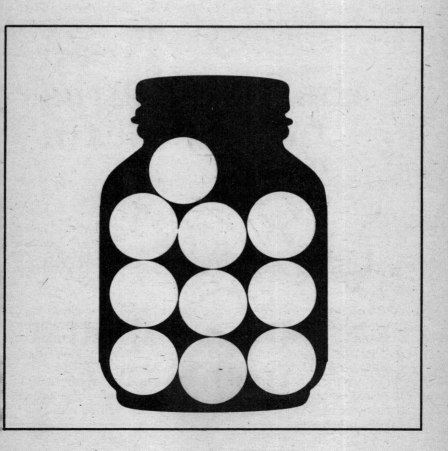

**read
the adventures
of Tintin**

**friend of all
from 7 to 77**

Cotton Wool Football

The players, divided into two teams, sit on facing sides of a table about 1·20 m (4 ft.) wide. A ball of cotton wool is put in the centre and, at the word "Go!", the children blow it so as to make it fly into their opponents' half of the table. The team that succeeds in getting it over gains a point (a goal) and the cotton wool is returned to the centre of the table. The winning team is the first to get five goals.

Mimed Advertising

Prepare a list of advertising slogans that contain some action, such as "Join the Navy and see the world", "There's a tiger in my tank", etc. Divide the children into teams of four. Each team mimes one of the advertisements while the others try to guess the name of the product.

*Magic Places

The children march round the room, in pairs, to some lively music. When the music stops, everyone keeps completely still, where they are, and the position of the "magic place" is announced. The pair nearest to it gains 1 point.
Naturally the list of magic places must be prepared before the start of the game. Here are some suggestions: the piano, the door, the fireplace, the window, an armchair, etc. The game can be repeated several times and the winners will be the pair who have scored most points.

*Where Are You?

Divide the children into mixed couples and get the girls
to sit down on chairs placed in a circle round the room
and the boys to stand behind them. The boys are then
sent out of the room and are blindfolded before returning
to try to find their own partner. In the meantime, however,
the girls will have changed places.

To make the game more fun, allocate the name of an
animal to each of the girls who must try to imitate the
noise her animal makes to help her partner find her. The
boys may speak but the girls may only make their
distinctive animal noises.

The boys can either come back into the room one at a
time or in groups. The game can either end when the
first boy, or group of boys, has succeeded in tracking
down the correct girl or girls, or when all the pairs are
complete again.

Obstacle Race

Put several objects on the floor all over the room—a low
stool, a bucket, an umbrella or any other small thing. A
player is then selected by drawing lots. After looking
carefully at the course, he is blindfolded. Without a
sound being made, all the objects are removed from the
floor and the blindfolded player (who knows nothing of
this, of course) set off round the room to cover what he
believes to be the same course as before.

54

Rally Racing

Divide the children into teams of four or five players.
At various points in the house, check-points are set up
which must be passed through in a prearranged order. At
the word "Off!", the first team sets out—they must do
everything prescribed in the first stage then run to the
second check-point and so on until they reach the
finishing line. Each team is timed with a stop-watch.
When all the teams have finished the course, the one who
has completed it in the shortest time is the winner.
Here are some suggestions for the "trials":

1 Each of the players writes his name, address and date
of birth (have the pencil and paper ready).
2 The players take off their ties and put them on again; or
they take off their jackets (or sweaters), turn them inside
out and put them on again.
3 The players run on all fours to a given finishing line.
The second player must not leave until the first one has
finished and so on with the third and fourth contestants.
4 Each player in turn eats three biscuits (one at a time)
and then gives the "Off!" to the next player by whistling.
5 Each one in turn opens a deckchair, sits down in it,
gets up again and then folds it up.
6 Each player hops on one foot, holding the other in his
hand, to a prearranged point, after which the second
player may start.
7 Each player runs to the next check-point, taking three
steps forward and two back.
8 The players are confronted by a suitcase full of clothes
—preferably women's clothes. Each player in turn must
put them on, run round a stool or table, take them off and
then hand the clothes over to the next player.
9 Each player is given four paper bags which he must
blow up and burst.
10 The players approach the finishing line by taking
steps that are only as long as their own feet; going as fast
as they can by touching their right toes with their left
heel and vice versa.

Travelling with the Alphabet

With the children sitting in a circle, ask each one in turn,
"Where are you going?" Each player replies in turn, using
the letters of the alphabet in their right order. He must
give the name of a city, county, town, etc., that starts with
the letter that he must use, and with the same letter he
says what he intends to do there. For example:
I'm going to Abingdon to ask Auntie's advice.
I'm going to Birmingham to bake bath buns.
I'm going to Coventry to cure calloused cows.
I'm going to Devonshire to drink delicious dew.
I'm going to Ebbw Vale to enjoy Emlyn's eisteddfod.
And so on to the end of the alphabet (perhaps omitting
X, Y and Z). If there are more players than letters of the
alphabet, you can start again from A. If a player is not able
to make up a sentence, he is out of the game.

Mr and Mrs Balloon

For each guest you will need an uninflated balloon, a
length of string and a felt pen. (There should be two
balloons of each colour, and it would be a good idea to
have a few spares in case any burst while being blown up.)
Put the balloons in a hat and let the children pick out one
each. They then have to blow them up and tie the
mouthpiece with the piece of string.
Now the boys try to draw a girl's face on the balloon with
the felt pen and the girls try to draw a boy's face. Then
the balloons get "married" according to their colour:
Mr and Mrs Green, Mr and Mrs White, etc., and a vote is
taken to decide who wins the prize for the most
handsome couple.

Proverbs

This is a game for which preparations must be made before the party. Choose a few proverbs made up altogether of about as many words as there will be children. Then take the same number of balloons of the same colour as there are words in each proverb (for example, if one of the proverbs is "A stitch in time saves nine" you will need six balloons of one colour), blow them up and write a word from one of the proverbs on each of them. When you have finished, deflate the balloons and start another proverb on, say, some red balloons. When the party has started, all the deflated balloons are jumbled up in a hat and all the players take one out. They divide up into groups according to the colour of their balloons and at the word "Go!" everyone blows up his balloon. As the players discover their proverb, they sit on the floor in the correct order of the words. The winners are the team to make up their sentence first.

The Advertising Game

Before the party starts cut out a number of display advertisements and stick them on to pieces of card. Cut off the names of the products and keep them on one side. Give each of the advertisements a number and hide them all over the house.

The players divide into two equal teams. Each player is given one of the titles and he must then look for the appropriate picture. The person organizing the game sits at a table waiting for the players to come and consult him. When a child thinks he's found the right picture, he must report back to the control table, show the title and say the number of the advertisement to which it refers. (He must not bring the picture to the table.) If he has guessed correctly, he goes to sit with his team. The winning team is the one to finish first.

Dancing Statues

Each player is given an empty container or a paper tumbler and puts it on his head, upside down. He must keep it there, without touching it with his hands, while he dances to music. Whoever lets his fall is out of the game. Every now and then the music stops and each child must stay quite still, like a statue, without letting his carton fall to the ground. This game can go on until all the players except one have been eliminated.

*Defending the Balloons!

Divide the children into mixed pairs. Blow up some balloons and tie one to a wrist or ankle of each of the girls. The couples then start to dance and the boy has the double task of defending his partner's balloon and of trying to burst those of the other girls. The prize goes to the couple whose balloon is the last one to be burst.

A Balloon Tournament

Divide the children into two teams who must line up, facing each other, on two sides of the room. Give some balloons of one colour to one team and some of another colour to the other team. At the word "Go!", the teams must cross the room, trying to protect their own balloons and at the same time trying to burst their opponents'. At a given signal the battle comes to a halt and the players go over to the wall on the opposite side of the room from which they started and play restarts. The winning team is the one which manages to keep the most balloons intact.

International Charades

Divide the players into groups of three or four. Each group must indicate to which country it belongs by miming any action representative of that country so that the other groups can guess the name of the country. For instance, the group that represents India might drape a sheet around one of its members like a sari; the group representing Turkey could pretend to be travelling on a flying carpet.

The Advertising Race

The players are divided into teams and each team lines up in front of a table. On each table there is a pair of scissors and a newspaper, pencils and paper. Give each player in each team the name of an advertiser which he must write down on a piece of paper. At the word "Go!", the first child from each group must run to the table, look for his own advertisement, cut it out, fold up the paper again, run back to his team and put himself at the end of the line, after first having touched the second player who must then set off right away to carry out the same tasks. The winning team is the one to finish first.

Thirteen Cards

The players divide into four teams—one will choose hearts, one diamonds, one clubs and one spades. Three stools are put in the centre of the room and one member from each team dances round them to music. When the music stops, the players fling themselves on to the stools but one, of course, will not be able to sit down and will have to remain standing. The other three are rewarded with one card each of their team's suit. It is then the turn of another four players and three of them will also win a card each. The winners are the team that is first to collect all thirteen cards of their particular suit.

A Very Pretty Thing!

This is a very restful game to play when everyone is tired of running about.

The players all sit round in a circle. One of them goes into the middle and is blindfolded. Everyone puts something that he happens to have with him on to a tray—hair-ribbons, rings, watches, necklaces, handkerchiefs, etc. One of these objects is put into the "blind fly's" hand while all the other children sing, in chorus:

"Here is a thing and a very pretty thing;
    Pray tell us the name of this very pretty thing."

It is usually easy enough to guess but then the children immediately start to sing again:

"Here is a thing and a very pretty thing;
    Pray tell us who owns this very pretty thing!"

The "blind fly" must try to guess to whom it belongs. If he succeeds, the owner of the object must take his place. If not, he is given another object to identify and the game continues.

Air, Land and Sea

The captain takes up his position in front of all the other children who are sitting in a semi-circle around him. He tosses a ball, or a piece of rolled-up cloth, to one of them and says *one* of these three words—air, land or sea. The player who has received the ball immediately has to give the name of an animal that lives in the element mentioned. Anyone who is slow in thinking of an appropriate animal, or repeats one that has already been given, or suggests an animal that does not live in the element indicated, is given a penalty point. When a player has accumulated three penalty points, he is out of the game and must pay a forfeit.

Ball and Spoon Race

This game needs concentration and skill.
The players split up into two teams and line up. In front of the first child in each is placed a teaspoon and a ping-pong ball. At the word "Go!" the first player in each line picks up the ball in the teaspoon, using only one hand, and runs all round his team in a clockwise direction (that is, he keeps his team on his right). If he lets the ball fall, he must start again from the beginning. When he has succeeded in getting back to the head of his team without dropping the ball, he puts it back on the ground, with the spoon, at the next player's feet—the second player will already have moved forward to take up his position. While the second player sets off, the first goes to the end of the line.
As soon as all the members of a team have completed the course and the first player is once more at the head of the line, all the players sit cross-legged on the floor. The winning team is the one which succeeds in sitting down first.

Romeo and Juliet

The purpose of the game is for Romeo to find his Juliet. Two players, who are Romeo and Juliet, are blindfolded. They stand inside a ring made by all the other children and, by calling out Juliet's name, Romeo tries to follow her voice when she replies. She may respond in a very low voice and then change her position right away. It is very amusing for the other players to watch the gestures of Romeo and Juliet who, without realizing it, often pass very close to each other.

The game ends when Romeo has won his Juliet and another couple take over.

Tick, Tack, Tock

This is a useful exercise to test the reflexes! The players sit round a table and must obey the captain who sits in front of them at the head of the table. The captain gives the following commands, in any order he chooses: "Tick!", "Tack!", "Tock!", "Tick tock!" and "Tock tick!". The orders have to be followed by beating on the table like this:

Tick!: beat with the palms of the hands;
Tack!: beat with the forefingers;
Tock!: beat with the backs of the hands;
Tick tock!: beat with the elbows;
Tock tick!: beat with the wrists.

The players must go on with one movement until another order is given. Any player who makes a wrong movement, is slow in carrying out an order or stops before time, is out of the game and must pay a forfeit. The captain of the game can of course make any movements he likes that do *not* correspond to his orders or he can repeat the same order to confuse the players.

1234
5678
9101112

Portrait Painter

Three to five children are chosen to be the artists and they sit in front of the rest of the group. Large pieces of white cardboard are put over their faces and tied behind their heads, thus completely covering their faces. They are each given a felt pen and must start to draw their own faces on the cardboard, following the orders of the master painter who will say, "Draw the left eyebrow . . . now the nose . . . now the right ear," and so on until all the features have been called out. The results will be more than amusing! The artists must then parade in front of their audience before being allowed to see their own self-portraits.

Analogies

Analogies are words that have some connecting link between them. For instance, the first analogy in the list below would go like this:

The *father* is to the *son* as the *mother* is to the . . . ? The object is to complete the space with the appropriate word.

It's great fun to read these analogies aloud (you can make up your own lists too) and see who is able to give the most correct answers. They should be read quickly so that no one really has time to think.

1	Father:	son	Mother:	. . . .
2	Foot:	shoe	Hand:	. . . .
3	Chicken:	cockerel	Goose:	. . . .
4	Pencil:	paper	Chalk:	. . . .
5	Cow:	calf	Horse:	. . . .
6	Hat:	head	Cloak:	. . . .
7	Sheep:	lamb	Frog:	. . . .
8	Balloon:	gas	Inner tube:	. . . .
9	Motorboat:	engine	Canoe:	. . . .
10	Scissors:	cloth	Razor:	. . . .
11	Bow:	arrow	Rifle:	. . . .
12	Bird:	nest	Bee:	. . . .
13	Wheelbarrow:	man	Cart:	. . . .
14	Horse:	reins	Dog:	. . . .
15	Sea:	boat	Sky:	. . . .

Answers: 1 Daughter, 2 Glove, 3 Gander, 4 Blackboard, 5 Foal, 6 Body, 7 Tadpole, 8 Air, 9 Paddle, 10 Beard, 11 Bullet, 12 Beehive, 13 Horse, 14 Lead, 15 Aeroplane.

Nose, Nose, Nose, Mouth

1234
5678
9101112

The players sit round in a circle. The captain puts a finger on his own nose and says, "Nose, nose, nose," while the other players imitate him. In saying the word "Mouth", the captain puts his finger on his own ear or some other part of himself to try and trick the other children who must touch their mouths. This is a game that should be played rapidly. If a player makes a mistake, he takes over from the captain.

1234
5678
910 1112

Monsters

Each player draws some object that can be made into the head of a figure, without showing it to his neighbour. He folds the piece of paper in such a way as to hide his drawing and hands it to his right-hand neighbour who then draws the body and folds the paper again. The third will add the legs and the fourth the feet. The papers are then opened up and, as you can imagine, the results are surprising.

1234
5678
910 1112

Animal Hunt

Write down the names of several animals and birds on pieces of numbered card (one letter on each card) and then put them around the room, each word jumbled up but clearly visible. The children will all have a pencil and a piece of paper and their task will be to re-compose the names of the animals and birds, writing down their names with the letters in their correct order. Five to ten minutes are allowed and the winner will be the one to have written most names correctly.

Here are some examples:

1	Rhinoceros	(ronicosher)	11	Robin	(biron)
2	Panther	(phentar)	12	Hyena	(anehy)
3	Elephant	(lethapen)	13	Giraffe	(frifage)
4	Beaver	(ebrave)	14	Gorilla	(lagroil)
5	Mouse	(umose)	15	Reindeer	(derinere)
6	Bullock	(clobulk)	16	Squirrel	(rilquers)
7	Sea-lion	(olianes)	17	Tiger	(grite)
8	Camel	(clame)	18	Dolphin	(phildon)
9	Cockerel	(creckole)	19	Zebra	(braze)
10	Leopard	(dropale)	20	Buffalo	(foulfab)

Memory Game

Put about fifteen small items on a tray—for instance a pen-knife, a pencil, a clothes-peg, a rubber, a teaspoon, etc. The children are asked to look carefully at these things and try to remember as many of them as possible. Now cover the tray up with a cloth and give each player a pencil and a piece of paper. When told to start, the players write down all the objects they can recall in five minutes. When the time is up, uncover the tray and call out the names of the items. The player who has correctly written the most items wins the game.

SSS
SSS
SURPRISE

TREASURE

TREASURE

TREASURE

Treasure Hunt

This game must be prepared before the party starts.
Wrap up some small presents (one for each guest) and
hide them in various places all over the house. At the last
moment, while the children are having their tea or playing
another game, attach a long piece of string to all the
packages. Take each piece of string behind pieces of
furniture, under chairs and carpets, etc., until all the ends
—each of which will correspond to a gift—meet together
at one point. When the children start their treasure hunt,
each one will follow the string track until it leads to his
particular "treasure". If the gifts for the boys are
different from those for the girls, it would be a good idea
to wrap them in different coloured paper or, better still,
tie a small piece of ribbon on the ends of the string so that
the children can tell at the outset which are for boys and
which for girls.

Animals

If more than six children are taking part, it would be
better to play with two packs of cards. Deal all the cards,
one at a time, face downwards.
Before starting play, each player chooses the name of an
animal for himself and is only addressed by the other
players, for the duration of the game, by the sound made
by his particular animal. To open the game, everyone
takes the first card from the top of the little pile in front
of him and puts it, face upwards, on the table. At the same
time, he looks at the cards the others have turned up to see
if anyone has a card equal to his own. If, for example, two
players have turned up a four, they must each make the
noise of the animal the other one represents—the one to
do so first wins all the cards his opponent has so far
turned up. It is not easy to remember, quickly, the noise
of the various animals, especially if it is rather rare and

difficult to reproduce as, for instance, the sound made by a fish, a frog or an elephant. The winner is the player who is left with most cards at the end of the game.

Telegrams

1234
5678
9101112

Select ten letters from the alphabet and ask the children to write them down on a piece of paper. They then have to compose a "crazy" telegram consisting of ten words that start with the ten letters you have given them. At the end of a certain time, which you can decide beforehand, each player reads out what he has written.
If, for example, the letters were SGWSPFQHNY, a player might write, "Send goloshes weather soggy prevents fishing queer happenings near Yarmouth", or "Seen Gussy wants seventy pounds flying quins home next year".

TRICKS

White Magic

1234
5678
9101112

Tell your friends you are able to guess any object they choose while you are out of the room. Your assistant, of course, will stay with the others. When you return, he will ask you, "Have we chosen . . .?" and will name, one after the other, various incorrect items. To each question you will reply, "No". Finally he names the chosen object and you will answer, "Yes". How have you done it? Immediately before naming the *correct* item, your assistant will mention something white.
Now change places and choose another object with the same friends. When your assistant is brought back into the room, start to question him in the same way. But this time, before asking him the right thing, name a black object.

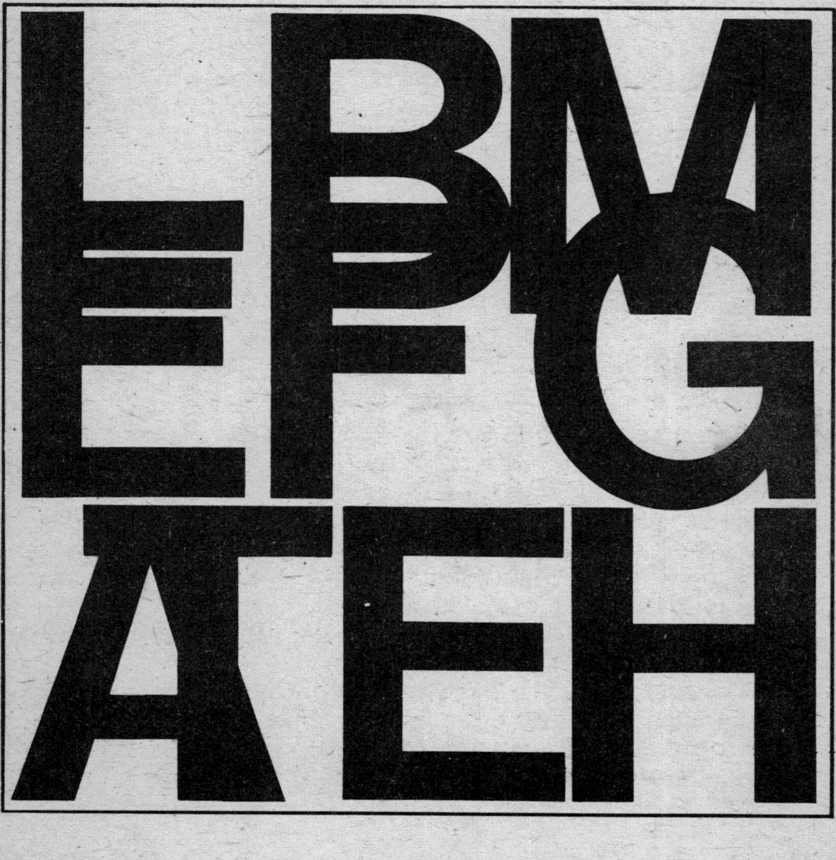

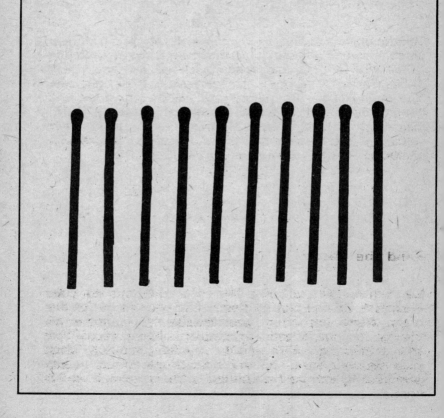

Guess the Number

Tell the children to choose a number while you are out of the room. We will suppose that the number 61 has been selected. When you come back into the room, your assistant lists a series of numbers, for example: 24, 32, 77, 61, 13, 80. The last digit of the first number (4) tells you that it will be the *fourth* number in the list which is the one you must "guess".

"Of course not!"

Tell the players to choose the name of a famous historical personality and then go out of the room while they decide. When you return, your accomplice will ask you, "Is it Julius Caesar?" or any other name except the right one. You must reply, "Of course not!" When you think it is about time to put an end to the game, you reply "No!" instead of "Of course not!". This will be the prearranged signal for your assistant to put the name of the chosen character and this time your reply will be "Yes!"

Find the Match

Lay ten matches out in a line on a table and ask your friends to choose one of them while you are out of the room. When you return, your assistant will point to all the matches one by one—in complete silence. You will be able to select the right one by watching carefully what your assistant does—he will indicate the correct match immediately after he has pointed to the last match on his right.

FORFEITS

Some suggestions for the redemption of forfeits:
1 eat a slice of lemon;
2 spell your own name backwards;
3 solve a riddle;
4 recite a poem;
5 tell a funny story;
6 count from 50 to 0;
7 hop round the room on one leg;
8 find the door in the dark, go out and close it;
9 mime a job or an action of some kind;
10 make the sound of an animal.

Games
for a day
ill in bed

CARD GAMES

Pyramids

From a complete pack of cards take out the four aces. Put the rest of the cards face upwards and make a pyramid by placing a single card at the top, then two underneath this, then three under the two, then four under the three and five under the four. When the pyramid is made, put two of the aces on the right of it and two on the left. Now try to put all the cards of the same suit on top of the aces, in increasing numerical order (i.e., 2, 3, 4, etc.), starting with cards taken only from the pyramid. Every time a space is made in the pyramid, fill it with a card from the pack. The cards that cannot be used either in an empty space or on one of the piles will form a discard pile and can be used to fill in the empty spaces in the pyramid when the pack is exhausted. The cards may only be dealt once—if you have not been able to complete the four suits started by the aces, using the cards from the pyramid as well as from the pack, the game has not worked out and you will have to start again.

The Clock

This game is played on the face of an imaginary clock. The player arranges the cards, one at a time, face down-wards, so that there is a little pile of cards for every hour and one in the centre where the two hands meet. When the pack is exhausted, there will be thirteen piles of four cards each.

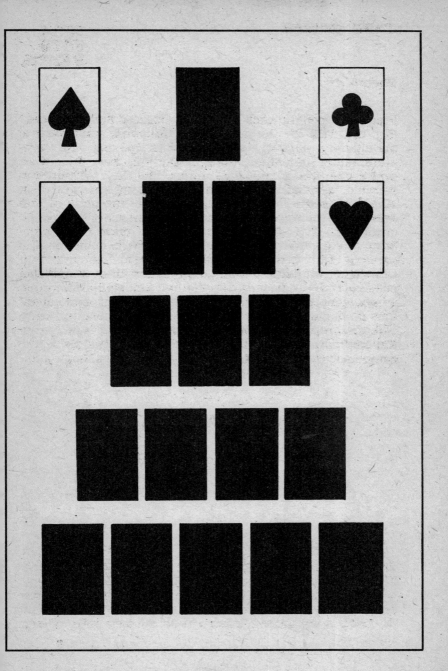

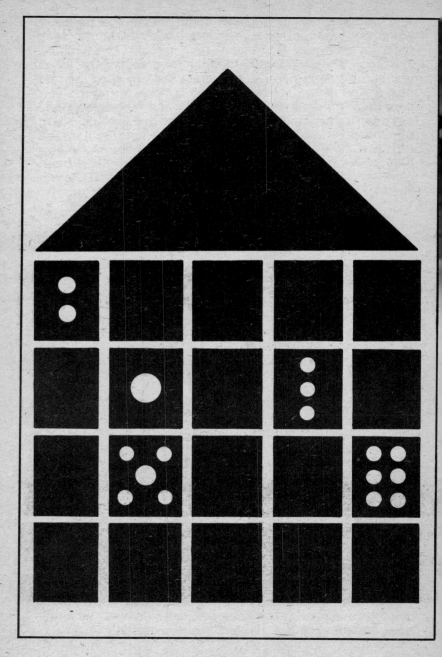

The purpose of the game is to move all the cards of equal value to their corresponding positions on the clock face: for example, all the aces on 1 o'clock, the twos on 2 o'clock, the jacks on 11 o'clock, and so on; the kings go in the centre. To arrange the cards in their correct places, the player starts from one o'clock, turns the first card up and puts it, face upwards, under the corresponding pile (for example, if the first card at one o'clock is ten, put it under the cards at 10 o'clock). Then you turn up the top card on *this* pile and put it under its corresponding time, and so on. In order to win, all the cards must be in place on the clock face before the kings in the centre. If the pile of kings is completed first, the game is lost.

Travellers

The travellers are cards which, arriving in an imaginary hotel, are looking for their correct rooms. A pack of fifty-two cards, after being shuffled, is divided into twelve groups of four cards each and placed face downwards in two horizontal lines of six piles. The four cards which remain should be put on one side for the time being. The idea is to bring the four aces into the first pile in the top line, the second pile to consist of twos, the third of four threes and so on, from left to right, up to the last of the second row, which will be made up of the four queens. After the twelve piles are set out, take one of the four remaining cards and put it, face upwards, under the pile that corresponds to its value (for example, if you turn up a six, put it under the last pile of the first row; if you turn up nine, put it under the third pile in the second row). When you have done this, turn up the top card of the pile under which you have put the card and place this one, face upwards, under the pile that corresponds to its value, and so on until you turn up a king, which must be put on one side. Continue the game until you have to turn up the second of the four cards that were left over, then the third, then the fourth. If the four kings turn up before all the cards have been put in position, the game has not worked out. However if the sequence of the four aces and the four queens has been completed before the kings have appeared, it has worked out successfully.

Pomanders

These have a sweet fragrance and are used to perfume clothes in the wardrobe.

Take an orange or a lemon and make a number of holes in the skin with a sharp pencil or a bradawl: they should not be too deep. Now stick a clove in each of the holes until the fruit is completely covered. When you have done this, tie a ribbon round it at the widest point so that, apart from decorating it prettily, it can be used to hang the pomander up.

GAMES WITH CLAY

If you do not happen to have any clay in the house, you can make some for yourself with a cupful of salt, one of flour and as much water as is necessary to make it malleable but not sticky. This is salt clay. It hardens slowly as it dries out, or more quickly if it is put in the oven at a low temperature. Any clay that is left over can be put into a plastic bag and kept in the refrigerator. The things that can be done with this material are endless. Here are two suggestions for making things:

Pearls

Make some little clay balls of different shapes and sizes and then make a hole through the centre with a toothpick or cocktail stick. Arrange them on a baking sheet and leave them to dry out in the oven. When they have hardened, paint them with enamel paint and string them on to threads to make necklaces and bracelets.

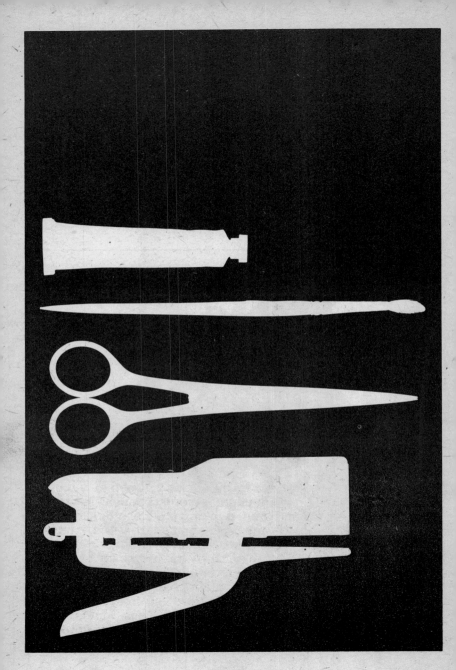

Vases

Work a ball of clay, pulling and pressing it until you have moulded it into the shape of a vase or jar.

Another method is to roll it into pieces about 30 cm (1 ft.) long, like a stick of liquorice or thin peppermint rock. When you have made a few, curve them round and round, one on top of the other, until you have made the shape you want. (The outside and inside must be smoothed out before baking so that the "sausages" have disappeared.)

1234
5678
9101112

Collage

Collage is a design made by sticking together various materials, such as crêpe paper, coloured paper, pieces of paper d'oilies, tissue paper, drinking straws, old magazine illustrations and greeting cards, pieces of fabric, cotton wool, silver paper, wire, pipe-cleaners, etc. In addition to materials like these, you will also need a sheet of cardboard, a pair of scissors, glue and a stapling machine.

Good results can also be obtained by cutting out the figures of people and animals from old magazines and putting them together again with arms, legs, hands, etc., positioned differently and arranged in the most unusual ways possible.

The Architect Game

For this you will need some squared paper, a ruler and a pen or pencil. Try to draw the plan of your room or of your home, to scale, showing the position of the doors and windows and also the furniture. The scale could be one square to 30 cm (1 ft.) if you are making a drawing of your room or one square to 90 cm (1 yd.) if you intend making a plan of your whole home.

Internal Telephone

If you have to stay in bed, a telephone can be very useful to be able to communicate with the other members of your family.

You will need two paper tumblers or two empty tin cans and a piece of string about 3–5 m (3–5 yds.) long. Make a hole in the bottom of each container, thread the two ends of the string through the holes and make big knots in the string so that it does not slip out. Cover the string with wax by rubbing a candle over it several times, after which the telephone will be ready to use. Be careful to make sure that the string is always taut and that it does not touch anything while you are speaking, or the vibrations made by the sounds as they travel along it will be broken.

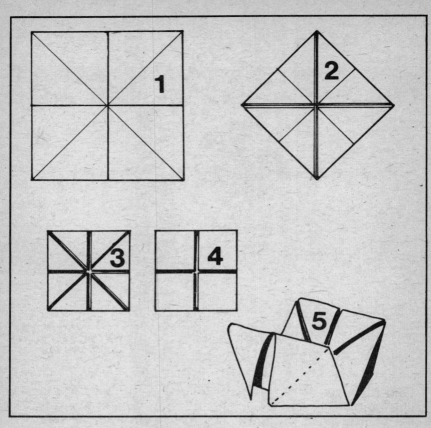

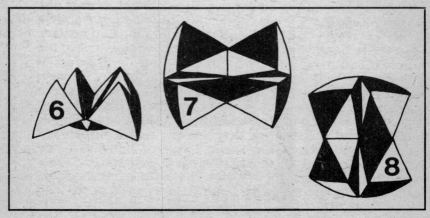

FOLDING GAMES

Heaven and Hell

1234
5678
910 11 12

Fold a square piece of paper, following the lines of the
illustration (fig. 1). Then fold the four corners towards
the centre (fig. 2). Turn it over and again fold the four
corners towards the centre (fig. 3). Now turn it over and
you will see that you have four little pockets (figs. 4 and 5).
Slip your left index finger and thumb into the two pockets
on the left and your right index finger and thumb into the
pockets on the right (fig. 6). Join the left-hand points to
the right-hand ones—this opening represents Heaven
and you can colour it blue (fig. 7). Now join the upper
points to the lower ones—this opening represents Hell
and you can colour it red (fig. 8). Move your fingers
quickly and you will find that Heaven and Hell open and
close alternately. Ask a friend to say a number. If, by
continuing the opening and closing movements to correspond with the number he has chosen, Hell stays open,
then he has lost the game but if Heaven stays open, then
you have lost it.

A Chicken and Her Chicks

Start in the same way as for Heaven and Hell (fig. 1).
Now unfold the piece of paper and leave the square in
the centre to act as the base (fig. 2). Bring the points in
the middle of the sides (fig. 2a, b, c and d) to the centre
(fig. 3). Bring points 1 and 2 down, as shown in fig. 4.
Now fold b towards a (fig. 5). Bring point 1 over to the
other side to make the chicken's head (fig. 6). Finish off
by drawing in the eyes (fig. 7).
Take a similar piece of paper and divide it into four small
squares to make four chicks (fig. 8).

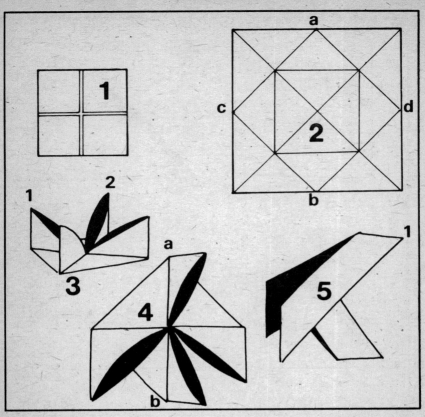

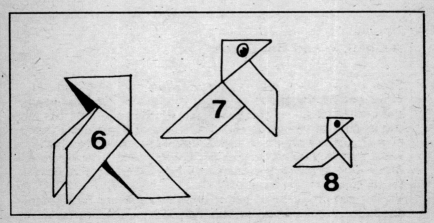

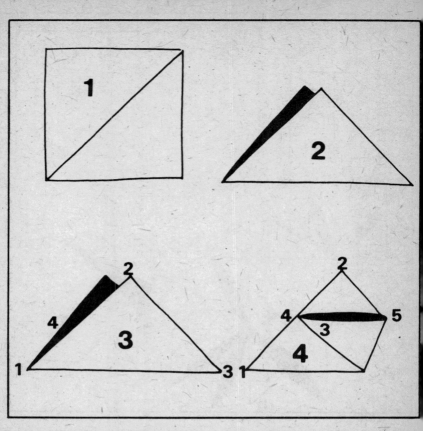

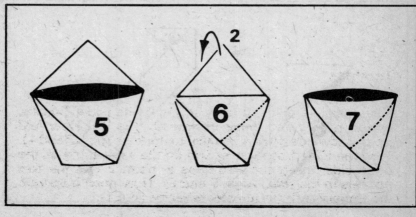

Tumbler

Take a square piece of fairly strong white paper (ideally, waxed paper) and fold it diagonally (fig. 2). Now fold point 3 towards point 4, parallel to the base (figs. 3 and 4). Turn the folded paper over and do the same thing on the other side. Insert the two flaps at point 2 into the two pockets in the sides (figs. 5 and 6). Now open it up with the fingers and the tumbler is ready (fig. 7).

A Dachshund and her Puppies

Fold a square piece of paper in four equal strips so that it forms an M (figs. 1 and 2). Fold each corner, from the top, on both sides, then fold points a and b towards each other. Now go back to the original M shape and fold corners 1, 2, 3 and 4 inwards (figs. 5 and 6). Bring point b over to the left so that it goes in the same direction as a (fig. 7), then fold points a and b in half, towards the right, to make the legs (fig. 8); do the same on the other side. Finish off by drawing in the eyes. You can take smaller pieces of paper to make puppies.

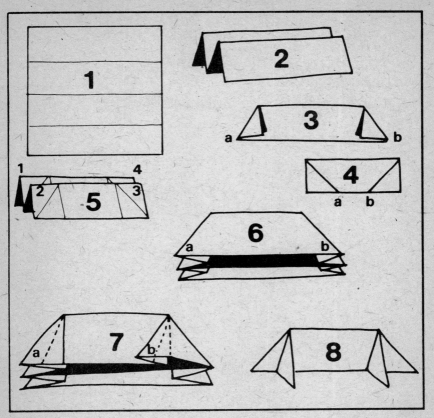

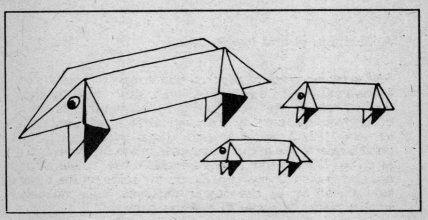

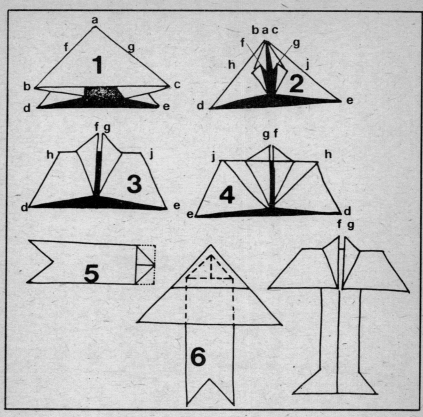

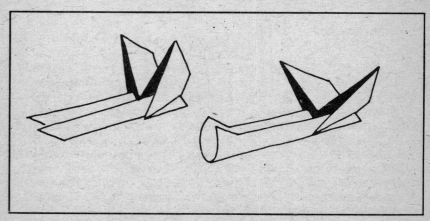

Aeroplane

Fold a square piece of paper in half then in half again. Unfold and fold it diagonally. Holding the triangular-shaped paper, fold each outside corner in towards the lower point, forming the shape in fig. 1. Fold points b and c towards a. You will now have two new points at f and g. Fold back bac (fig. 2) underneath a line hj to make fig. 3. Turn it over (fig. 4) and the wings of the plane are ready. Now take a fairly wide strip of paper, fold it lengthwise and cut the tail (fig. 5). Open the fold, bend back the two corners at the top and insert the strip as in fig. 6. Your plane is now ready for flight.

Windmills

Fold a strong, square piece of paper or cardboard as in the illustration and cut it into four squares (fig. 1). Fold each of the four squares diagonally (fig. 2). Now open them up and cut along the fold line starting from each corner and cutting almost to the centre (you might like to draw a small circle in the middle of the square and use this as a guide as to how far to cut and to ensure that you cut the same amount from each corner).

Put a large-headed pin (a drawing pin will do) through one of the top corners of each segment in turn (marked with dots in the drawings) and then through the centre (fig. 4). You will find you have made a four-pointed star (figs. 5 and 6).

Fix the windmill to the top of a stick or on one side of it (fig. 7). Now run with it and see how your windmill whirls round!

You can also make double and triple windmills, with multi-coloured paper. The centres of the windmills can be decorated with stars of other colours (figs. 8 and 9).

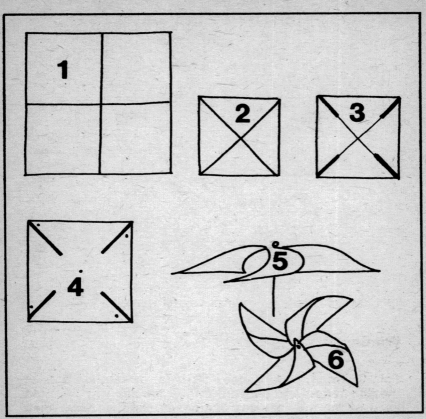

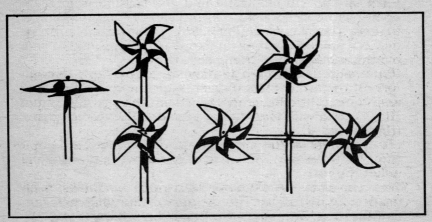

Index

INTRODUCTION

GAMES FOR A CAR JOURNEY

Animals and vegetables   12
Who lives there?   12
Time and distance   15
Animal hunt   15
The route official   16
Word splitting   16
"If he were . . .?"   16
Names of   19
NUMBER PLATES   19
Numbers in order   19
Choosing a number   20
Word making   20
The alphabet   23
Letters and words   23
Proverbs   23
Car identification   24
Make and date   24
Story roundabout   24
Botticelli   26
The beaver   28
Signs   28
The sleeping giant   31
Treasure hunt   31
The ghost   31
The box   32

PARTY GAMES

What is my name?   36
Country, city, river, landmark   36
Months of the year   39
Mysterious hands   39

Twin ribbons 40
Journalism 40
Car identification 43
Topping-up 43
Balloon race 43
Catch the whistler! 44
The sculptor 44
Cops and robbers 47
Blow-ball 47
Bean race 48
The flying puff-ball 48
Cotton wool football 51
Mimed advertising 51
Magic places 51
Where are you? 52
Obstacle race 52
Rally racing 55
Travelling with the alphabet 56
Mr and Mrs Balloon 56
Proverbs 59
The advertising game 59
Dancing statues 60
Defending the balloons! 60
A balloon tournament 60
International charades 63
The advertising race 63
Thirteen cards 64
A very pretty thing 64
Air, land and sea 67
Ball and spoon race 67
Romeo and Juliet 68
Tick, tack, tock 68
Portrait painter 71
Analogies 72
Nose, nose, nose, mouth 75
Monsters 75
Animal hunt 75
Memory game 76
Treasure hunt 79

Animals 79
Telegrams 80
TRICKS 80
White magic 80
Guess the number 83
"Of course not!" 83
Find the match 83
Forfeits 84

GAMES FOR A DAY ILL IN BED

CARD GAMES 86
Pyramids 86
The clock 86
Travellers 89
Pomanders 90
GAMES WITH CLAY 90
Pearls 90
Vases 93
Collage 93
The architect game 94
Internal telephone 94
FOLDING GAMES 97
Heaven and hell 97
A chicken and her chicks 98
Tumbler 101
A dachshund and her puppies 102
Aeroplane 105
Windmills 106